Baffling Gravity

By the same author

Poetry

Lives
The Caught Sky
The Flower Industry
Brushing the Dark
Album of Domestic Exiles
Russian Ink
The Islanders
The Unmapped Page – Selected Poems
Tremors – New & Selected Poems
Speed & Other Liberties
Fuel
The Lives and Times of the Islanders
The Bicycle Thief & Other Poems

Essays
How to Proceed

Anthologies
First Rights – a Decade of Island Magazine
(with Michael Denholm)
Toads

Baffling Gravity

Andrew Sant

PUNCHER & WATTMANN

in association with Shoestring Press, UK

Published by Puncher and Wattmann
PO Box 279
Waratah NSW 2298

http://www.puncherandwattmann.com
puncherandwattmann@bigpond.com

A catalogue record for this
book is available from the
National Library of Australia

ISBN   9781925780239

Cover image, 'Pigeons', by Alan Dixon

Printed by Lightning Source International

This project has been assisted by the Australian Government through the Australia Council, its arts funding and advisory body.

Australian Government

Australia Council
for the Arts

Acknowledgements

Poems in this collection have previously appeared in *The Age*, *Antipodes*, *Art Monthly*, *Blue Giraffe*, *Australian Book Review*, *Australian Poetry Journal*, *Best Australian Poems*, *Island*, *Meanjin*, *Poetry Review*, *Plumwood Mountain Journal*, and *The Weekend Australian*.

I am indebted Rosalind Holinrake's *Clarice Beckett and Her Circle* consulted prior to writing 'Plain Respect for Clarice Beckett'.

I am grateful to the Australia Council for a grant during 2014/2015 and to the University of Kent, UK, where I was RLFWriting Fellow in 2015/2016.

ABOUT THE AUTHOR

Andrew Sant was born in London in 1950. He emigrated in 1962 with his parents to Melbourne where he completed his formal education. He has lived in London at various times, particularly during the last decade. During this period he has been a Writing Fellow at the Universities of Leicester, Chichester, London (Goldsmiths College) and Kent. In 2001 he was writer in residence in Beijing, China at the University of Peking. In 1979 after moving to Hobart he co-founded the Tasmanian-based literary quarterly Island and continued as joint editor for a decade. He has worked as a teacher of literacy to prisoners and the unemployed, of English to non-English speakers and of humanities subjects to students in mainstream institutions. He has also been a copywriter and a manager of a hostel for juvenile offenders. He is a former member of the Literature Board of the Australia Council. His essays have appeared in the annual *Best Australian Essays* anthologies, and a collection, *How to Proceed*, was published in 2016. In 2003 he was awarded the Centenary Medal. He now lives in Melbourne.

Contents

3: Gravity

1: Gravitational Pull

The Tilers

Three of them, nailing down
    a geometry of slate. I'd be sorry
if they move on soon
    to some other leaky London roof.
I hear them, five storeys high, opposite,
    tap, tap, tap, over and over
like someone trapped under rubble, news,
    a catastrophe, the future of cities,
they don't count on beneath
    a Constable sky. They banter.
One sings 'Blue Suede Shoes'.
    I admire their footwork.
They don't look up as I do,
    from the window,
with a cultivated eye. Sensibly
    they look down—Euclid's their guy—
placing exactly each slate.
    Pitched roofs are a forecast of rain.
I look up, as if for the tilers, at the sky. Hmm.
    Maybe I'll have quit town, zipped
my bag, flown south before
    they've finished their expert resistance.
I'd be glad, though, to stay
    till they go, having viewed their roof
with as little gravity as I do
    a pavement—as I whistle
some old hit perhaps—exhibit
    a walker's brisk equilibrium, go
nowhere that stirs up vertigo.
    The tilers resist its attacks, exist like cats.
They show, startlingly, to those
    with a level nose for doom,
hey, that thing is never going to happen.

Meteorite

Maybe it was the streak
    of light in the night sky
some kid in a hinterland
    called a falling star   opportunity
for a wish   maybe it doubled
    as a portent in the direction
of a priest   maybe it dropped by
    at 10pm local time
exactly   without doubt
    suddenly a hot rock   aeons
of momentum making certain
    it would be a special museum
attraction   very welcome   not often
    thereabouts to have the honour
the paying of respects by outer solar matter
    no knowing firmly where it's
been hanging out in exile
    since the scandal gangs of macho
cosmologists call the Big Bang   some trip
    the bulk of the narrative
missing   dark energy now
    ever in the background
a barren planet or two perhaps
    a cautionary feature   no guessing
how complex before the ore-laden rock's
    what-the hell-is-this-entry
into the rare atmosphere   spectacular
    with lots to offer a full stop

A Comparatively Old Window Pane

Decades without quaver
                              it's still fine
the pane can't make up its mind
which side to be on

and peering through,
                              taking opposite
points of view, I collude—

it simply takes no position; amply open,
therefore, to be wiped
and be shined

while I happily practice
Buddhist detachment.

Set glass still flows. No it doesn't, Heraclitus.
As is proper, the heated opinions
are firmly divided

by glass. Nor—spare me Voltaire—
can I see, no matter
how long I've stared

through the pane and
regarded a transparent
harsh fact,

that it will ever shatter or crack.

His Equilibrium

To run is an advance on regular walking,
an early lesson. Hear the cheers at the finishing line.
It both gets you closer and farther away, a kind
of balance. Our species, newly upright, steady,
demonstrated this on the savannah, made it
out of Africa. Often, frankly, I too can't wait
to make escapes. Still. No way I'll get soaked.
We singular bi-pedal primates like to range.
When sedentary, we bloat. Predictions were I'd one day
race in the Olympics. But who likes training?
It's a more serious challenge to maintain balance
in motion with both eyes closed, a feat involving bodily
centre of mass, and big toes. Progress slow. Older.
We're each a clocked experiment after heading off.
Unless toppled, in gravity's remit, at full throttle.

The Man Who Loves Useful Sports

As a boy
he played cricket
badly, wickets quickly
dashed; afternoons wasted,
the point of them, missed.

*

Not a competitive step
did he venture
onto the football ground
without dissing, even at the brink
of victory, the merits of team spirit
to anyone near the boundary
who'd listen.

*

If all talk
was a sport, he'd be less
of a walker.

*

As for golf, he shares
for the game the disdain
of Mark Twain who knew,
when he saw it, a good walk ruined.

The uses of the lone
three iron he owns
have yet to be proven
on an agile intruder.

*

If ever he feared
his ex-wife would shoot him—
jumpy after her fun at the gun club—
such a rapid execution
might with telescopic accuracy
have been viewed
as the fallout
of a killer sport he's
known to approve.

*

Though he's yet to shoot
an animal for food, he is a hunter—
the quarry, lists of enticing ingredients, as he follows
a tricky recipe's every move.

*

Without weapons in the house
(or a wife), he's reassured to learn
it's likely a while yet,
on the stressed and pressured planet, before
the lack-of-resources wars.

*

If he behaved
less like a gunner, he'd be more
of a runner.

*

When he begins struggling
to swim, floodwater
rising—he's read the Bible—
it is he alone, no
team player, who'll surface
from that recurrent dream.

*

Then he labours to know
the appeal of watching, in competition,
the strenuous butterfly stroke.

*

Don't mention lacrosse.

*

On the other hand, yachting
at limited cost ...

*

Not a tycoon in sight,
nor a celebrity or crew,
paparazzi or sky-high mast,
among many, therefore
not a marine view of boats
in Monaco or Barcelona—
just our man, picture this, his back
to all that excess,
cross-legged, attendee
of a modest regatta
and fresh from performing
an exemplary breast-stroke;
mentally afloat, he composes
an agile, roving, maritime ode.

At The Hotel Splendide

There's a broad view of the sea
and key fobs are made of mahogany
at the Hotel Splendide.

Remember? Maybe not.
It may not be possible.
The five-bladed fan, mechanical insect,

in the dining room had possibly stopped—
out of consideration
for the weather, cool from hot—

and all the better to fix it
in mind. Time there never
is pressing. The staff are forgetful.

In the Hotel Splendide
the staff are discreet. For each passing guest
a private balcony's empty.

The four floors, the corridors,
the grand atrium with its Steinway piano
and calming palms are often mute

as a hospice at dusk
for the rich in *dishabille* or whoever's
attendant blood roars on.

There are cocktails at the cost
of leaning high on a balustrade
between midday and nine.

None soon will remember.
Witness the mirrors—
the mirror ornately framed in the hall,

the long mirror in the lift,
the mirrors, two in each room—
the wardrobe, the dresser—

another, man-size, propped
for an epoch against a wall; mirrors
oval, oblong, and mantle ...

You can see, stepping past yet another,
the Hotel Splendide
is dedicated only to recalling itself.

There's a bold letter 'S'
in the antique tiles at the entrance,
on each fresh serviette,

and those who stay duly remind
themselves in the mirrors—
repeatedly—of actual guests.

Stranded Cactus

This cactus looks as if, on a reef,
it could be neighbour to sponge, equally at ease
under the sea—or strange as some tentacled hydra
on the window ledge, free
of quickening leaves.

Giant-sized, in a desert, the colossus
fingers, uplifted, would look fine
or finer at sunset for being
in stark silhouette.

Thus no necessity to have the expanse
of the Mojave up close,
mesas, mirages, scree
—the ocean of sky which eagles grace—
and here also there's aridity;
the cactus in its pot
surviving neglect, and now
rain, a deluge, smiting
the window, not a drop
to seriously bother the indoor climate.

Who cares when its yellow
flowers on long stems pouted,
craving some insect plentiful perhaps
in the Grand Canyon! Yet

it always proceeds, stoically;
and when the house
was re-opened, the cactus was still left alone
as, earlier, the telephone.

                              For how many
millennia did its genus try
successfully to evolve utility spikes?
and now not a nosy predator in sight
while, root and stem, the cactus absorbs
available moisture. Thrives.
                              Admire it,
serial neglecter, and its tiny
needs—a bagged ocean
sponge was never as domestically
clever as this, if squeezed.

Truly Among the Hoodoos

Cappadocia

A multitude, as far as I could
first see, shocking exclamations
of rock endlessly reflecting
one another, it appeared, in a sort
of appalled fascination. Clearly,
I repeated, they can coach students
of geology by rote—tapering
afternoon shadows lay down
the same daily points. They're a conical
arsenal making a late blow
against erosion, spooky in moonlight.
Truly, they look like a giant
gathering of the Ku Klux Klan.
Come dawn, tourists board hot-air balloons
in a brave attempt to get the clearest
perspective. But how many, stunned,
come down in flames? The place
is obsessed, one beige cone abruptly
after another—strolling admirers
beside them so tiny—are a show
honed from compacted ash thrown
out of an upset volcano which quit
doing its one spectacular trick.
What a singular attraction! Early
Christians, persecuted, burrowed rooms
in the hoodoos, and boomed. I scouted
about freely, long shadows casting
doubt on any choice way out.

Quarry

Where the quarry you've come across
    was once, its nitrate explosions,
bulk rock thumping the ground,

wonderful shudders long over—
    and the gut masculine satisfactions,
the foundations for Federation houses

well settled, backgrounds perhaps
    for the remotest family photos,
faded, lost or boxed-up anonymous—

eucalypts have long taken root
    in the jagged artificial cliffs,
their damp fissures and cracks.

We might say they 'cling' to the cliffs,
    thinking of ourselves, looking up,
as being precarious

beneath the afternoon sunlight
    the trees distribute. These
or any species you see

are mostly invisible, namely
    how they were before now,
how they'll become awesome

to others, possibly in moonlight.
    Wherever you find yourself there's
only time, a little or a lot, to glimpse it.

Gravitational Pull

Gravity always proves itself:
the climber falls, the pen drops;

an angry lover slams a door,
a glass topples off a ledge and shatters—

a constant, the gravitational attraction.
Gravitons, though unobserved, make sense

should they be there, blind
to Einstein's theory, defiant.

A wall collapses, a meteor
brightens the night sky. Balls of unequal mass

it's reported Galileo dropped
from the Tower of Pisa, a high

Renaissance demonstration, peaked
in a dead-heat. Equally,

when gravity makes sediment impressive,
the bedrock might well be reckoned

to express weight in falling, spent.
Newton explored the force, mostly indoors.

Only a featherweight
without room to exist in a big vacuum

could possibly make light of it.

The Multicoloured Ball in Motion

Kicked, the multicoloured ball
brightly defies prevailing weather,
cool, damp, windy. We,
the small boy and I, observed by those
in cars on the promenade,
are the beach's sole performers.

We compete for possession, the goal
is not to boot the ball into the sea
although to lift the game out of the bounds
of safety I sometimes kick
so that the boy will see the risk
of a ball afloat and chase it.

He sees the danger, exhibits mock distress;
I'm gentle with the ball, an easy fetch.
The boy grins, boots it back to me again
to arc, maybe, toward the promenade.
I'm sure that should his ball roll
to the water's edge, wavelets

will ride it back into simple reach—soon
this is proved true, the people sheltering in cars
perhaps amused by the speedily
averted threat. I guess they assume
the boy is related to me—he's already
lost a football, gravity the recent hauler.

This new one, and the game, now benefit
via managed risk on the beach
side from catastrophe. It's about the size
of the standing globe of the Earth
in his home, the ball—a world to the boy
running for it where the sand is wet, finally

not quite keeping up I see, elsewhere
on the beach. Hard to tell from there
if my daughter has passed on
any trace of me in his features but it's clear
the multicoloured ball is now
at the water's edge and with steady

momentum moving past the wavelets
as I thought it shouldn't in any way but is
and should, it's obvious, produce
salt tears and singular action,
the sea, as I wade into it, soon deeper
than the height to which I've rolled my jeans,

no feeling that the water's cold. The orb
in motion resembles, it quickly seems
in its isolation, a floating planet
out beyond me on the water—
and one, in a young boy's eyes,
viewed with distant, uncertain hope.

The fully-clothed man he watches, now
waist-deep in the wide sea, a diminishing
figure, might well be thinking
how unwittingly big risk may begin,
the boy exposed in wind to the actions
of his elders—freshly evident—among

the first to view the NASA photographs
of the pulsing Earth, newly shown
as small, unique, exhaustible,
taken from, as a wading man
now seems from a bobbing ball,
a relatively astounding distance.

The warm people in the cars look on.
From their vantage through
rained-on windscreens, the man's
modest prowess (to also rescue
family genes from deep foolishness)
gets their localized attention.

It's all or nothing. The tall, bothered man
will be soaked through. Hard to believe, they see,
that what he saves is all, a common ball.

A Nude Not Forgetting a Photographer

for Jane Burton

The photographer is pacing
around her Cylcopean
camera on tripod. She can't
take her eyes off the time. The nude is late.

*

4pm. The nude in disguise—
t-shirt and jeans—
divests it, emerges
whitely, smooth as a baby.
The bench on which
she'll stretch her Venus
perfection is blemished by lichen.

*

When the camera's positioned and ready,
the nude rolls a cigarette.

*

In spite of the qualities
that make her a suitable nude
for this particular shoot,
she is an awkward nude.

*

Torn between mentioning
the discomfort of lichen and the alteration
in the weather, the nude yawns.

*

The photographer raises a finger and shouts, 'Hold it!'

*

This is a nude
with lassitude.

*

(A nude reclining
on that hard bench would be better cushioned
if she'd been selected by Rubens.)

*

The photographer lifts her eyes
to the darkening sky, impatient,
realises again that time
is her professional element
and in it hopes now
or soon, in the viewfinder,
in the last of the light,
call it Roman,
she'll see,
as will others in some
stylish interior, a co-operative nude.

*

Forever out of the picture:
the nude and the photographer
rapidly
adapting
to circumstances.

*

As if to stress
that being naked and being a nude
are not the same,
in response to her subject's statement,
'It's bloody freezing,'
the photographer, mistress
of illusions, says *sotto voce*,
'Don't worry, darling, it won't
show in the photos.'

Mr Habitat the Anticyclist

To you, idle bike, on this positive day
of light wind resistance, my pledge,
as always, is for motion—and to curse
inertia. How could I possibly resist?
Your every brand-name feature commands
my servile obedience—
bright bell, shiny pedals, stylish lights.
Most people agree, you're a super machine
that surpasses the car when an owner comes
to being mastered: I sweat like a wrestler
ascending some patient Himalaya;
on the level, head down, I punish my legs;
in the rain I get parched and wet—
only a pro would think he's in charge.
Freewheeling fast beside traffic, I submit
meekly to risk—and on tricky gravel.
It's your carbon neutrality that argues
I'll go far, faster, and always wins
as I weave through queuing cars, do
what cars can't with two wheeler agility.
Which makes you, hyperbike, a remarkably
hard driver—as any safely amazed
bystander surely sees. Balance,
in a tight jam, I have it! You're master,
I'm servant fit to denounce the negative
agreement. Seat requires drying, I speedily wipe;
leap on, in a storm, my uniform
attire deletes me. Who's gleaming?

To Charleville

for Leah and Tom

The overnight train journey to Charleville
not taken remains a sadly
forsaken opportunity. What difference
it would have made, what discoveries
might have occurred along the way,
I cannot know. For I refused to fork out
the excessive fare—a week's wages
for many a labourer—to reserve a designated seat
and sit up all night, rigid, as if attending
a remarkable lecture. At the Toowoomba station
I did not make an enquiry about the price
of a sleeping compartment. The train,
that night, would formally depart without me
and, I was told, most all of the seats
I could choose from would be empty.
This, I said politely to the man
in uniform, I can understand.
                              The journey
not taken could have been to an outpost in Ethiopia,
or one on a Russian steppe, or to some
other destination I'd lately researched,
a consequence of having personal business
in the region—some unvisited place
the locals don't consider to be remote,
an isolated cluster of lights
maybe seen from a plane at night—
but, on that recent day, it was to Charleville, Queensland
I didn't set forth with a flask of soup and a desire
to feel unleashed from care, acquire
whatever wisdom might come about
from travelling to a town where once,
in the main street, a man, deriding gravity,

fired cannons at recalcitrant clouds
in the hope of breaking a lengthy drought.

The expensive overnight train journey to Charleville
remains with me in past prospect—the vast
canopy of stars from the windows, the rhythm
on the rails of wheels, the meditative
journey with a fine excuse, like some
fabled island, to make it. Or, actually,
two supermarkets, three butchers
and two bakeries, the official website states
as attractions—and better still
'No one should go hungry in Charleville'
which skinny millions, jammed into carriage
after carriage, would applaud if they could ordinarily
make the trip. I was better off without a ticket.

Expecting the São Jacinto Ferry

The ferry, red contra white, was long delayed,
no reason offered. The sea was calm. Reflections
from the quay and boats periodically ran deep. Sunshine
was intermittent. Then, ropes released, the ferry left.
A half hour direct to São Jacinto, away
from the idle cranes and freighters; herring gulls whining.
This happened last April, time for the ferry to moor, its steel gates
parting for the residents and their small cars. Stray visitors.
The broad resurfaced esplanade—in sports track ochre—
was soon again deserted except for men, ex-sailors maybe,
sitting around an outside café table. Shadows
of the postcard palm trees were fan-shaped till cloud
erased them. Doors on the little balconies of the portside houses
stayed shut, the sea a clear disappointment. A visitor
would not seek to ask why the Esplanada Bar was closed
but wonder at the need, like a final insult, for the sign that says
ATTENÇÃO Proibido Pescar to tempt old
fishermen to be disobedient. The ferry left
to eventually reappear, always now too late to connect
with industry. On the Rue Dos Estaleiros the deco ship
equipment factory stands a wreck, windows all teeth, smashed,
gravity of the financial crash littering the dark interior. Other
monuments to past employment approach collapse,
roof tiles gone, walls cracked. No-one, or no-one visible,
except a stranded visitor, was fascinated or alarmed—since
what's happened to the folk around São Jacinto cannot attract fair,
satisfactory understanding—by the men dressed in black, from boots
to balaclavas, who raided the ruins,
spilled out, weapons tilted (more strange emergency aid
from the European Union?) an actual Portuguese
commando attack—on whom?—or gun theatrics in anyman's-land,
the enemy not then in April a brand of sunny economics,
the exercise complete in time for the troops' conveyance
on the afternoon ferry, late, as expected
by the gloomy and gutted in that or any other month to come.

The Night Journeys

Nightlights strobe through the window's
    condensation, signals from anywhere, a stratosphere,
        at 3 or 4am—sometime to find oneself suddenly

awake, making haste across a country
    that will forever contain others' breadth
        of residential moonshadow. Or an owl's. The train's

motion is all; sleep the only known border
    when travelling through such space. Then slowing to a halt,
        somewhere as gripping as grease, wheels seizing the rails,

as if a reason to continue on into the long night
    is duly being mustered, a wearisome matter.
        Sleep, then. The resumed rhythm of the train under stars

is a drug big pharma can't ever market.
    Horizontal, on a bunk, the idea of levitation
        gets close to how abandoned by gravity

the body, an addict, feels—where?—between
    a distant foreign point of departure and a vaguely
        understood destination. The train ticket admits

one traveller to erase hard distance itself,
    then memory of it. If transmigration is release, a vast belief,
        this surely must be like it, once, then repeatedly.

Time, Embodied

Olive oil, rice, tea;
a bottle, a bag, a packet—

I'm linked to the calendar
days, weeks, months

by the sum of disparate
ingredients, as the user who's

reducing them, say, an inch or two
of honey yet to be spooned.

I comprehend the heft
of time as I pour,

in this temporarily
leased small apartment,

from a big bottle of Filippo Berio
extra virgin olive oil

to cook a pasta dish mixing
chilli, garlic and anchovies,

or I lift the fat bag
of Yutako rice

in which time surely
is also embodied. It is a longing

that verifies this.
Time weighs heavily. Gravity

might help dash the bottle
of Napolina balsamic vinegar

but would make no impact.
Time, obdurate, simply

won't be appeased
by hourly offerings

of Twinings tea.
The ritual is, sparely, mine alone.

Each of these brands,
dwindling slowly, foreshadows

how much—if anything—
will be better to have left

in excess and, finally, chuck.

2: Baffling Gravity

Tamarillos

Vertigo is nowhere
where they are, and time,
too, seems suspended.
Ovoid, working on ripeness
dozens make no demands
on the branches, light,
they might be, as blown eggs,
easily out of reach among
the sunlit leaves. Tamarillos,
tree tomatoes, *tomates de ârbol*
or whatever name holds them aloft
in a nation's esteem, these
exotics, close to the window,
are merely mute absorbers
of birdcalls and banter,
no-one's gift to cuisine;
a slow over-the-summer
accumulation, providing
silence with a shape
like a form of percussion
never to be struck.
In their plenty they are polished
and smooth experts
at deferment, unusually
snobbish. Elsewhere, in rows,
they're a crop. The
compelling force, it's
beneath them to address,
they hourly thwart; another lofty
thing that makes the fruit look
so perpetually good—
who'd wish to pick any?—
until the first one drops.

Source

1

Shifting, the source of the river begins
in run-off and seepage, far from here,
a forested upland; the named and un-named
tributaries to its south-east concede,
at each confluence, to the Yarra, its downflow,
at this place, in late summer, steadily slow.

Call the river's course 'progress',
which it offered when, on the north bank,
a colonial mill pounded; the first inhabitants,
around the valley, by then haunting a silence.

All the global water that's flowed since Dight
built his mill goes smoothly over his weir.

It was never intended to be, but is, soothing to hear.

2

The perpetual sound of water falling
intensely, yet what the sandstone cliffs
make of this place has memorable depth, its source
the sediments trapped four-hundred-and-twenty
million years back, give or take some, under
a Silurian sea.
                        The strata look fresh, neatly
layered, undulate like long waves.
The motion of the uplift caught, it seems,
by the afternoon light, next to the river,

well above the lost ocean it's come clear of;
journeying creamy rock—lightweight enough,
given a little tectonic force to do
the hauling—an epoch shown, in a squeeze.

3

As it happens—causality nascent—a saxophonist
stood, when eventually spotted, at a high confluence
of geologic and historic time, on the cliffs
overlooking the river.
                              His instrument glinted, tiny.
Shirtless, he shone. The low notes flowed, as if
a far off source informed them, then rose some distance—
the sound of the water falling close to those few
who heard him, improvising, like the course of a river.
He sought no audience, no more than does a Silurian uplift
and what it expresses. There seemed a pureness in this—

the source of his music restorative, liquid, breezy as cliffs.

Change

for Tina

The guy who lately dated and initialled
himself into the sandstone foreshore

knew what is coming. I stood
where he crouched, scraping hard, became

oblivion there decades ago, no mark
to signify summers spent within range

of the boatshed and jetty. The other side
of Beach Road, the reliable houses, we, the truculent

youths of the day, moved out of
have taken the cue. The showy new, mansions

of the deluded, bully their owners.
I owe a debt to the cliffs, robbed them

of fossils. Beyond repair, the jetty.
I forget the name of a girl—urgently

we gave the planks a shake. Mostly
there was fishing from them. Spare, idle days.

I thought, by now, I'd be long dead, be over
poking among rocks with more absorption

than when looking for something lost, but then
I never had, on the edge of the bay, a heron's

patience. Stationary, the one I saw
in the shallows that windy day I went

back made a fixture of the present tense.   .
The bigger fish we went for, shark,

came wrapped with chips in recent newsprint.
JFK was dead or else last week's weather

absorbed the grease. The same shop, among
the multiply exchanged, still fries fresh fish daily.

Greater surprises are kept from affecting
the arriviste real estate—and I'd see no harm

in honouring the woman who pulled her little cart
with its paints and brushes past the endemic gossips,

with a plaque. Clarice Beckett's timber house is history.
Her paintings, once recovered, made and remake

a lasting asset from this brisk location
of aesthetic space. A working place

forgets its citizens. Beneath the cliffs
where fossils of the late Miocene are spotted—

seals, penguins, bones of whales, species
gone extinct—I dawdled until I saw the heron lift.

The Predators

The airport lounge, another
waiting room, is filling—

women in track pants and sneakers,
guys, lofty, in baseball caps (though
no baseball soars around here), men,
anxious with iPads, in smooth suits, bespoke
for the groomed politician moving swiftly through
to the exclusive and aloof Flight Club rooms.
Seats, facing rows, few now vacant—
crisps, with fizzy drink, brittle and spilled;
kids sleeping, the place a squeeze
for the obese. A waiting room

more capacious than most (but those directed
to hospital Emergency know better),
seething impatience released,
as to be expected, in a crowd restless
about being constrained so long after
the checks for explosives. Submissive
within limits, within a certain ignorance
like animals herded
and penned, fright
not yet exciting them.

A gut hunger to be gone
shoving all through the crowd,
in waves, the male floorpacers fuelled
by delays; a predatory directness
on their faces, or frustration
(it's tough to be the world's greatest
predators, caged), and not far off,
never, from exhibiting murderous rage.

Mosquito in Amber

Mosquito, this is where I'm glad to find
you, trapped in amber,
proboscis not able to push
into my skin. Now I'm quick
to admire your anatomy, flashy
as flying specimens I've recently slapped.
Head, thorax, abdomen,
perfectly intact; wings'
immaculate crossveins possible
in the lit museum case to spot;
the compound eyes, feisty antennae—
and giant legs saved from parading
a parasite further into her prime.

But even better, mosquito, in spite
of our closeness, is the complete absence
for me of itch, swelling, angry rash,
guaranteed by the eighty-million-year-old
confinement of anticoagulant saliva—
making it dreamily comforting
you've been here to stay since the Cretaceous
unable to drift, primordially
whining, in and out of my sight.

Mediterranean Time

The swarthy plumber who sets a time
to fix the taps never comes. Water
drips in nearby limestone caves
with less regularity from stalactites.
Church bells clang, now in a frenzy,
then once only and, much later, once again—
shuttered solitude now in silent streets
during the heat of the afternoon. In the shade,
on dusty ground, thin cats yawn.
Hibiscuses expose their sexy throats.
Should the plumber come, after
a siesta's done, he'll likely find
no-one home. He may later phone.
The sun shines hard on a limestone landscape
from which, block by sawn block,
the villages have risen as did—but how?—
megaliths during the Neolithic.
There's no division of colour, honeyed,
between what's man-made and the land—
the villages often atop the coralline-
capped mesa-like formations.
They look down on tiers of ancient cultivation.
Olive lizards spurt in and out
of drystone walls—a species
endemic to the island after the sea
gushed into the Mediterranean basin
with cataclysmic swiftness.
The Romans called the landfall Gaulus.
Its stratified cliffs are the Miocene
made scenic. Marine fossils
in a fanned museum line up
under glass, put a contemporary shine
on geologic time; another case displays ancient bones.
Perhaps of a distant, distant forebear
of the plumber who, in this farrago,
shrugs off haste, short north of the cliffs.

The Gozo Public Library

Books that might never be shelved
teeter in high piles on trestle tables—
in this library it's a chance find
that must satisfy.
                    Here, in the half
light, how quick I am to reflect
upon sedimentation, accumulation,
stratification—the worn-out books,
older than the average reader,
slowly melding.
                    Not far off,
I've strolled solitarily along
a sunlit cliff top, layers of hard
limestone on a coastal bluff, to the west,
worth comprehending,
gradually.

Impossible to read the slow
alterations, the odd donations
since last I visited this public library.
The term used for the durable limestone is *globigerina.*
In some future epoch
the sea might win it back.

Maybe there's a neat reference
to that sedimentary rock
I can't predict among the many
hard and soft disintegrating spines weakly
spared from heavy summer heat.

In brief: countless words are going under.

The budget permits one listless librarian,
a single fan. It's breeze, the cool offshore
kind for sudden readers, few, in pursuit,

with intrepid eyes, of lasting books.

Above the Equator

What's so appealing is how like and unlike home this place is—
whatever the trial idea of it has formerly been. Here the summer skies
are cloudless, week after week; at night, the flat roof is a becalmed
ship to walk on, the stars as guides. Do we, as a species, feel so alone
that the appeal of microbial life on one of Saturn's moons might
provide us with relief? There's no requirement, if so, to leave 'home'
to summon exile. Some days it might be handy to guide a robot on a
necessary local mission. Our moon has proved to be a disappointment,
except as a force. The rise and fall of tides here are small. Mauve
jellyfish pulse as if in gravitationally neutral space—beautiful on
a calm day; dangerous to dive nearby. The sting is the stroke of a
lash in a sea that's cool aquamarine. The mark of having visited
might otherwise come from remembering strange, trad music heard
through curtains, from an old house, which stays in mind as lastingly
as a tattoo—a scorpion or skull and crossbones on a swarthy biker
whose wheels meet soft bitumen along a cart-wide street, like news.

Musophobia

The trap I'll set is not the kind
that kills. Once a byre,
now a modern kitchen in a sixteenth-
century farmhouse, home
lately to a mouse, I've been lured in
to do the deed, perform a role.
The rodent has a lot of scope
to scare the resourceful, metropolitan
woman who's rehabilitated a ruin.
She shows me her view
of the Mediterranean. Wherever
she rests her feet the creature
streaks. Both woman and mouse
want to eat in peace. I haven't
heard her scream but this,
she assures me, is guaranteed
when they both make each
others' interior location known.
It took a lot of forethought
and courage to wrest this house
from the natural forces intent
on making hewn limestone
into stubborn rubble.
The mouse now has the power
of both architect and heavy
lifter. It looms. Transfigures.
When the woman lies awake,
it's huge. There's not been room
for both of them—and now
too much to dispatch my,
an actor's, ill-concealed surprise
at its fabulous size, the actual trap.

Mood Piece

Hung out on the line by its tails,
the white shirt drips as if
a rainstorm has passed through it.

The sweat has been rinsed out,
now the shirt displays forgotten
weather—its outstretched

sleeves seem to implore
their owner and the hot sun
to rescue it from vertigo.

Who could not fail to see
how dazzling, soon,
the dried shirt's become,

gymnastic in the welcome breeze,
a model of appealing cotton,
baffling gravity, no hands.

Prickly Pear

Taller than a man,
its tangle of branches
are a duplication of oval plates,
fat, swollen with sap—
if there's a loner throwing
shade, by the road,
there'll be a rabble
of others close by, wrestling
for space on an embankment
or entrenched, as if
dispossessed, on wasteland,
sealed by genetic necessity
against noonday heat.
Kill this cactus, this spiky invader;
as if out of stark shadows
it has massed, there'll soon be
reason to notice
from a high window
it's suddenly back—
and now, in September,
the fruit of these brutes
is ripe. Mind the spikes!
Call it prickly pear
and a nuisance or, hereabouts,
baitar tax-xwek*
and respected, its
status semantic, fruit
shaped like a grenade—
the packed seeds, bittersweet,
boom in the mouth.

* Maltese: 'spiky fig'

Abdul and Son

Prime time for chance encounters,
it was mid-evening among people mixing
beside the harbor in summer Mytilini.

Abdul, I wonder how close or far
you are from the hoped-for destination. Already,
when we spoke, weeks away from Damascus

and then two days more of fleeing
inland from the coast—the inflatable dinghy
abandoned, with the rest, thus adding briefly

to the broadcast number of refugees—
you're now to me a man released
from the statistics. You and your son, Odai.

Yet, back then, to be processed, fitted
with identity papers in a military camp,
the two of you living in limbo on the street,

like the other hundreds, interchangeable,
the evening huddles within view
of the restaurant tables' falling numbers.

Within their range, that evening, in one
of those chance links that lead passing strangers
into an exchange—you limping, aided

by a black walking stick, your young
son understanding not a word you said in English—
swiftly brought into focus rubble

of the bombed family house. Abdul,
I'll never meet, in passing, your wife, the other
children still, as you said, safe within a Turkish camp

except, as a Syrian teacher of English, in your
description. The subject of the stray bullet
that didn't lodge but passed through

your body expressed right there by
the allied stick. I'd framed a tricky question on
our first encounter. Now I wonder which borders

you may have crossed, with or without any
chance material help—north, following
the sea passage, toward Macedonia, then,

as quickly, without a backward look, Serbia's
immediately in the past, Hungarian villages soon
to note and forget. So, in brief, you hoped.

Each crossed for what may befall in northern Europe,
your chances. Somewhere, an open door.
The treatment, needed. That last time, in fading

light, I found you, watchful on a public seat,
I'd spotted next to it, from a distance, a boy wildly
waving a black walking stick in a made-up game.

The Pianists

At St Pancras Station, the pianists
step anonymously out of the crowd to sit
and strike the keys of its three pianos.

The trains are leaving by the minute
for Dover, Paris or somewhere closer.
The pianists themselves get up speed,

or go slow. Daily, weekly. Pass one or two
or pass all three quickly—if each
piano's active—and you'll encounter swift

refreshment, jazz, classical, avant-garde,
wide apart under the station's massive arch,
amid loud announcements. Why don't the pianists

race like us commuters to get to necessary
places, go off to get ill-paid? They've
arrived at a spacious oasis; no-one,

in a hurry, knows for how long
each will stay out in the open, playing.
Terrorists might appear and strike there,

the patrolling police show. They get to hear
the tunes all day. Its news will be
sensational. The pianists are elsewhere.

The Queues

Elsewhere queues are forming,
faces eager, anxious, subdued—
it's approaching midnight or
perhaps 10am. Many at length
will be turned away from the Alhambra
but not, mid-afternoon, from a cinema
in Chicago. Cold rain falls
or the sun repeats, hour after hour,
its heat, and the queues are orderly
for now, up to a point, and typical
like those which expected buses
in wintry post-war London, no-one
shoving (or conversing)—civil
compliance, far off in time and place
from a stampede for a train,
the men's teeth stained
with betel leaf, the too few places
already taken. Today
I queued, without incident,
to pay for groceries, so the fine
phenomenon is freshly with me,
the patience, the small expectation, relief
and, with time aplenty to reflect,
exposed mortality, personal death
moving ever closer, banal to all
other shoppers as an old joke.
To die in a queue might
it seems prove easy. Most flow
slowly, straight or meandering,
ancient human movement—will climb
the Great Wall of China, skip
modern Rome; approach giant telescopes,
drawn to outer space, equally endless.
Wend down, during a war, towards

a tight border-crossing or,
under a big sky, crisis food relief,
unless, like an angle of repose, frozen
gravity, a queue's noisily breached
as in a landslide, perhaps
a geo-political tipping point,
the screaming factor. Breaking news:
the tired, the tested, the trapped
of all nations think, *Screw queues!*
except for those in which each person waits,
remotely, that end up for them
where their helpful queues began.

What's in the Brown Cardboard Box?

Heavy, to a weakling, as rocks;
light, when set down, on the fit
floorboards—a mystery
removed now from storage. This, I know,
since I packed it: there are traces
of me gathered within, in the darkness, sealed.
Each strip of packing tape, as I rip
makes the abrasive noise the wake
of a fighter plane creates. This
is a violent entry: I'm taking the box
and contents by surprise; see,
when I open the flaps—hold them back, to look in,
as if for a ghostly former self to be freed—
I can be a bit of a Freudian gentleman.
For what purpose? A lot, at first sight,
of odd and ends. A box of HB pencils, a gift;
some inherited watches that long ago stopped;
a wrecked address book; an ornamental
bronze dog—each reminding me,
in the hard light, of why they were
trapped in a box with the other objects I lock
eyes on. Their weight is psychological
not standard—greater
when the swift invasion has fizzled.
With the exception, at last,
of pocket binoculars
I don't need to free from their case
to recall the wild worlds, green-leafed,
bird bright and brief that can't possibly

wait to be vividly close up again.

3: Gravity

Stamina

The long road itself,
bisecting the horizon, scant
trees beside it, advances a plan
for stamina. You stand there,
shadow across the planet.
Out of necessity you stayed
in that airless dump
with its bleached curtains, an age
but remained, like the window,
unbroken. The fat historical
novel was exasperating
until the penultimate chapter. How
does a spider, so readily
quick to act, stay spot frozen
for, it must seem, an epoch?
It's an enduring lesson.
You've lived longer, much,
than once you thought possible,
a wrong hunch, and now,
distant, know it's time
for breakfast again. Oats.
A sprinter by temperament,
in the event no-one said,
pal, it is a marathon.
This inner resource, like granite,
long ceremonies or speeches, bombs
make strong, brags many
universal applications. Local
gravity has it, despite cracks.

Machismo

Love hit
Billy, the kid, hard

though it barely
slowed his appetite
for wild oats.

That is, his guts
felt like porridge.

Let's spoon, she moaned
domestically, in bed, and they dozed—

sorely missed breakfast
if they overslept.

The kid, a thin legend
in his own mirror,
was constantly struck
by her touch.

Double

Correct house, number nine. He pays
the taxi driver. Alights. Forgets his novel
with the spooky cover. The door's ajar.
He pushes it open with his bare left foot.
It's the heat. The southern hemisphere sun
is blinding. The hallway, as usual, is dim.
He flips a lightswitch, notices on the table
the set of keys; looks up, sees
on the ceiling a large huntsman spider.
He knows the species has eight pairs of eyes.
He straightens a favourite picture many times,
calls out 'Katy'! Waits. Then calls again
and once again, before fetching up her image,
blue coat, scarf, loose hair, gloved hand
waving as his train glides out of cold,
echoing Frankfurt station. She weeps.
The bags he's set down beside his sore feet
are his alone. He thinks he's seeing double.
In the back room, a sash window
is open. Curtains motionless. Nor is it right
the phone, cut off, is suddenly ringing, ringing
or that in the kitchen sink is a flotilla
of soapy dishes. And who is the tall stranger
he now through a doorway sees
seated at the table, oblivious, reading?
They face each other, fleetingly. Phone gone silent.
'I'm here to live', the reader reading coolly says.
This threat makes no waking sense.
Nor is it lessened when in a mirror
—wedding present—he notices, looking
sidelong, the profile of the intruder
is the ruthless mirror-image of his own.
He sweats. He needs further room to move.
'When inside the house,' he at last rebukes,
'at least take off your shoes.' He'll
double check next time he's passing through.

Penderyn

Penderyn, the whisky, not the name
of the village I drove to,

I mean when I praise it.
The distillery lavishes its produce

with metaphors, a verbal Eden, but I'd suggest
my opened bottle is in the vicinity

of resembling to the taste
a twist of astringent toffee with a hint

of something aged in the Carboniferous,
offering brisk side-effects.

I arrived at speed in steady Welsh
autumn rain three hundred and fifty

million years after limestone
sediments beneath the village settled at great depth.

With a filter of such proportion for spring water,
the enormous dark whisky barrels,

with their malts, now take an Age
to absorb it. Or that's how it looks.

Should the grey village ever be minus
the distillery, it will instantly shrink.

Gravity

Crockery slipped in front
of Sammy's mum
as she faced the bench—
cups, plates. Then,
empty-handed, she'd run
her fingers through dark hair
and swear. Earthquake,
well, something beyond
our knowing was happening, the smashed
crockery everywhere. Sammy
and I got far away, smoked
contraband fags, confided. His mum
scared him badly; his dad
could be seen in remote
places interviewing people
on the BBC, a floating
situation on the concave screen.
He wore a trilby. To Sammy's
mum the kitchen floor
must have seemed wavy.
She poured nips of something
into a glass, and partly missed.
Sammy shinned up trees, hot
for rapid action, barely stopped
till he fell or gashed his legs.
His mum paused as she leaned over
gravity's small vortex in the kitchen sink.
Sammy had two younger siblings,
witnesses, and a cat. When
Sammy's mum, out shopping, walked
smack into a glass door it split
her stomach open; down,
she gushed too much blood to live.
Sammy collapsed one day after school

from a heart attack.
His dad, in black and white,
had nothing much remarkable
to say into his microphone
when the sound was turned up.

The Suicide Note

Public Records Office Reading Room

i.m. E.M.S.

That first Sunday afternoon
in September, the day
the doctor and the vicar came
and then the police,
you became incorporeal. Now,
half a century later
I read their names, associated
with a body, in pursuit
of their professional duties. Soon
you were everywhere, like the weather
and then, season following season,
I had no mind to leave
you behind; dreams, those
that afterwards linger, still
contrive to find you alive,
slender, hair greying early, pale—
as on the day I followed you
to frolic in a near freezing, clear
Lake District tarn—
but not, as I mentioned
to First Constable Reynolds,
without colour. Father,
as I formally called him
in the Witness transcript, was listening—
and in addition, I recall,
drawing on his pipe. Nor
does the First Constable impolitely
record his response to our pommy
voices, mine unbroken,
father's as if weaned
from the BBC, neither

about to break out
of constraint in the book-lined
study, like what remains
of a family from some gaol.
Did the First Constable sit on
the notion, behind the desk,
there might be something tragicomic
going on, an odd foreign
matter, before his sceptical
Australian eyes? This mob
getting off to a bad start
at improving their lot. He never
would be in time to catch
me crying. I confess, belatedly, I did—
whether or not the Cuban Missile Crisis
or a particular new sixties
pop masterpiece from Home
was linked. You, mother,
who till that Sunday made me
say my prayers and ask
forgiveness for my mischief,
uncontrollable in your mind,
could not escape the crazy
stigma, magnified tittle-tattle,
damning the mentally unwell,
exposed like weakened beasts
trapped for an easy kill—
could not forgive yourself
for the black trouble, in a strange
bright country, stalled for a while, now
stalking you again; another
institutional bed assigned
and ready, no getting away after all.
Perhaps the dislocation
ensured it. I've thought so,
ever since I was left
to do the talking, ever since

I learned of your psychosis
following my birth. So you wrote the note.
Then the taboo was broken.
Now I have before me, freshly,
the Proceedings of Inquest,
30th January 1963, a copy—
following my right to read it—
which, insignificantly, improves
my memory of First Constable Reynolds,
his pen and paper, though not the events
I could now better express
and extend his patience, therefore
best left, with the original,
in State storage. There it's been,
till now, terminally unrequested; ever
to be read by me at a future date.
But why so late? Not because of any
great foreseen distress when reading
in the Depositions what the First Constable
extracted from his cautiously
tractable witnesses—quizzed
the quiet husband and the quiet boy as,
later and at length through
subsequent decades, I'd persistently
want the truth, the personal history
however skewed by far-flung
relatives; get them eventually to blab.
Though I wasn't ready, even yet,
to find that father, pipe in mouth,
had already indrawn, like smoke,
emotionally damning evidence. Full
exhalation might have made
the young First Constable pale.
Nor could 'Found dead in bed'
or 'Overdose of barbiturates', the terse
words of the pathologist
find me lost for words again.

The words I didn't dare
to cope with are your own.
Those in the final note, that brief
form that prefigures bereavement—
the gravity of them never
meant for me to later read
or relate, in your familiar hand,
distinctive as the crinkled skin
on your elbows, when your arms
were loose in a summer dress.
Words the First Constable discovered
and, after father examined them, filed
away on the notepad page
as evidence. I leafed cautiously
towards it, then read
as if the ink was still fresh
and it's not too late to intervene,
came to my senses, and spoke
in that public reading room under
my breath to you, as I began to,
so long ago, beside your bed.
Until, when steady, I looked around
at others bowed over pages
and wondered what led them at last
to intercept the past, seeing none
were any longer young—clues
perhaps to old family cover-ups,
or even acts where, as typed
for the First Constable, there are
'no suspicious circumstances'.

Now and Then

for Trish Sinclair and Dugald Sinclair

A grandfather clock announces
the hour. Upstairs, the little girl,
chin in hand over a book,
hears it. Six. The pendulum,
patriarchal, is in full swing. Time—
it's early autumn—to run
outside, past, in his study, door open,
her dapper papa at his desk.
Although he, too, has heard
the steady registering of the hour,
as no doubt has his wife,
he's not in full accord
with his time and place. His daughter's
footsteps, a lone explorer's in the hall,
fade to naught. She's found a way,
past the precious roses—closing
her eyes to sniff the scent—
to climb, via an outhouse
and a metal downpipe,
onto the roof. So very high
up on the tiles, she chooses not
to look down, arms spread wide,
balance kept, progressing, until
she's straddling the sun-warmed apex.
Practice doesn't thwart the thrill.
How could she possibly imagine, almost
ninety years later, defying gravity
with a walking stick, she'd
be thrilled to recollect this? The man
next door, with a window view
of this derring-do, would choose
to doom it. He's of his time
in 1928, can't possibly see

what a shameful loss it would be
for a girl of ten to miss a secret
sunset flowing over Port Phillip Bay.
He's shocked to see her. He tries
a speech. The father receiving it in the garden
is attentive, patient, adjusts his tie.
He advances his thought. Next day,
the clock clangs four, five, six
beyond the hall. The neighbour,
window open, stares at a long ladder,
only an adult, a man, could shift
now propped beside the next-door wall.

Woman in Izmir

Armenian or a Kurd, I forget. Blue eyes, yes.
A Kurd therefore, I guess. Such a tested life
or death matter. She changed the sheets
and cleaned our room for the next guests
in the Hotel Antikhan. Izmir blew hot
through the open window. She took away
the drained water bottles. Her head scarf
was maroon, that's certain. Downstairs,
beneath a wall clock, time had stopped
in a wide, high-angled, framed shot
of Smyrna: commanding buildings,
a square, monument, the Greeks
still in occupation. That modest
hotel where the woman works, quaint
in the re-named city, had by chance
escaped acrid, revengeful flames.
A deliberate spark of one kind
or another—it remains unsettled—
started the conflagration. I expect
the woman, shy of foreigners, lives
in one of those hot architecturally
brutal Turkish apartment blocks, complete
with a fire-escape. A husband, kids.
We left for her on the dresser
some cash and a packet of apple tea,
little enough, as thanks, and unexpected.
This also is conjecture, a long shot,
one thing acting on another in a city
beset, too, by quakes and tremors:
she took the items on the dresser,
bought something extra, better, slowly
steeped the tea to its full sweetness
and, that evening, breathed in the home
atmosphere high up in their apartment.

Lucretian

The roof of the house has never fallen in
exactly, though cause and effect
are rife around here, gravity
especially persuasive.
                           Someone's limping.
Seek to be calm; to avoid
disturbance—death (not dying) being of no great
concern—is the aim.
                           Athens is in strife again.

Crunch that apple, suck that peach.
Next year the crops may well be wrecked.

There's much to be said about the weather
when it's not benign, lightning
fracturing the skies, the more the better—
a gift to the atomist attending to the sum
of things, his mind detached from that tricky
sub-atomic mix within the orbit
of particle physics. Ungovernable
as romantic love.
                           So listen,
although nowadays we fill the Void
with noise, diversion, surface chatter
or still, unbelievably, some Almighty, beyond
nightlights the silence remains immense.

Elsewhere, between sheets, is another
place to tune in to the heartbeat
affirming a chance conception, yours, the best
unambiguously good news around,

needing only, to approach it, modest shoes.

The Great Ocean Road

A trail of ants
for five days now pursuing
the same strict route, progress
rapid in both directions, thousands
travelling within my line of sight,
at all hours I notice when I'm nearby,
presumably having found
a booming food supply to feed the pupae
in their nest but who knows
where that grows either

and I'd appreciate
their fine industry more
if it wasn't happening
across the kitchen floor—praise the wonderful
logistics of it, large-scale co-operation,
the assumption that here's
their right of way, before I take action.

I suppose the floor must so appear
since the procession extends
with insistent confidence—
and there's no evidence
it's a fresh human food supply
the ants are plundering.

If a road provides
a right, across open country
or along a coast, for traffic
to speed upon it, no consultation
possible with the previously dominant
species of the region,
who's to question
these worker ants, ceaseless
in their duty?

From many thousand metres up,
through the window of a plane,
cars en route for hours or days
(such is the available space to take in)
clearly resemble the activity
that I witness in the confines
of the kitchen and consequently think
how much better it is, time
permitting, to progress
at ground level.

The ants, inevitably about
half their number, are heading
in a south-westerly direction
just, it hit me, like the traffic
going to Lorne or Apollo Bay
on the Great Ocean Road, cut
into the Cretaceous sandstones
of the area, loyal mostly
to the coast

as are the ants to pheromones
no longer now a necessary guide to the route
across the kitchen tiles.

It's summer, clear skies
and I'm driven to recall from experience
on the ground, car windows down,
what it's like to be riding
between remainder forest
and the ocean, the sense
of heading west and,
from that immediate perspective,
the liberating immensity
of sky, land, sea—the radiant
ocean vapour and, later,
wave after advancing wave making a glassy arc,

offering a sense of orchestration,
then breaking with a low boom
into lucent foam along the northwards
shifting sedimentary coast,
now a couple of thousand miles
free of once vastly treed Antarctica,
an aeon for species to accrue new features
very slowly, the sea working
and now reaped by surfers,
together making this long road
a continuous hazard
for any driver whose attention roams.

Ooooh! trippers go, their cars
clearing a hidden bend, as they sight the cool blue
and breadth of the ocean. I have
done so myself, one of what might be
a barbershop quartet rehearsing
a fresh harmony. So occupied,
and with the prospects of wet immersion
on offer, the mind ejects,
like refuse left for scavengers—small
black insects for instance—ominous
news and analysis, prognoses
and photos, the possible ever
lengthening personal witness statement
concerning inharmonious
activities, species collapse
and so
annually on,

together with evidence now near
at hand, away from salt air, which persuasively
shows that among the deluded candidates
who might next gather (are ready!)
to inherit this Earth, rate the ants.

A Photographer Not Forgetting a Nude

In her t-shirt and jeans
the woman clearly is not yet
a nude—a bother
for which the solution
is a proximate photographer.

*

The photographer shows up,
late, on the rocky foreshore, desolate
except, usefully—soon—
for a nude. Between
the hirer and the hired,
the upright and the reclined, now
stands the imperturbable tripod.

*

The photographer's CV is extensive.
The nude's ever pending.

*

(The ranging photographer
knows she for one
is not interchangeable.)

*

The rocky foreshore
is an accommodating background,
water rippling, space
for the recumbent nude
who's in her element, and where
the moody photographer

sweeps her eyes to
find a necessary
correlative.

*

Even when it appears the photographer,
atop Triassic rocks, is lost
in her imaginings of a geological epoch,
it's a naked Homo sapiens
not a beautifully evolved nude who wants to be off.

*

The stroppy photographer
subscribes to glossy *Aperture*
and peruses it, incognito.
The nude joins a group.

*

When the photographer calls
repeatedly
this particular session
a shoot,
this nude in particular
is prone,
somehow tectonically
time and again,
to be endlessly compliant.

*

The more the tall photographer is composed,
the less the short nude supposes.

*

At last, the extreme
contrast between
the smooth nude
and shattered sedimentary formations
she's now front of
in stark afternoon light
finds the photographer—
perilously angling her
Leica from a height—

                    on balance

a rock steadied shot.

The Inland Sea

A work by Rosalie Gascoigne

Inland being months away
from the littorals of the nineteenth century

European mind and a man,
Charles Sturt, on horseback

kitted out for the search. Why,
this far south—in a continent

which has dreamed up fanciful animals
with pouches and bounce

and egg-laying mammals—
would there not be a stretch

of water to place on the map shining
beyond the next arid horizon?

Rosalie Gascoigne, artist
explorer of jettisoned weatherworn

manufactured materials,
found, as if locating a mirage

in the corrugations
of roofing iron elevated

in a grid-like arrangement,
the jolting embodiment

of what, in all risk,
was not there, a missing perspective.

Plain Respect for Clarice Beckett

The cliffs where Clarice Beckett painted
are little changed; on a cold day
the beach could be free of people
as if in 1933. Her father's house, once
nearby, has long since been replaced.
Daily, she got away from it at dawn
and dusk, released from being the dutiful daughter.
'There goes Miss Beckett,' the curious
Beaumaris neighbours likely said,
seeing a woman, then forty-six, make her way
in any weather along the street
to see what only she could see,
and in her solitude perhaps enlist
the brief attentions of those informally
chancing upon her at the beach or near cliffs.
Beside her she had a little cart
for her equipment, a topic, possibly,
of gossip. It too was lost along
with much of everything else she made.
But that's not yet happened when
a neighbor says, 'There goes Miss Beckett,'
hearing from behind a hedge her cart,
if clipped hedges then were there in the sandy soil
I recall weeding as a youth when local
or any memory of Miss Beckett had been erased.
The suburb was always exactly well behaved.
Along her street I walked without a Beckett fact.
She no longer youthful arrived with her parents
in 1919, I as a lad with mine in1962.
I'd like to have been acquainted
with the artist, her life and paintings,
early on, the way she tonally expressed
the presence of the place with detached engagement,
the paintings as quiet as the isolated painter
(though she must have been well-spoken)—

a car disappearing on wet Beach Road,
early morning haze, lingering bathers,
the numinous light always diffuse in scenes
caught in the midst of change. I'd say
she painted quickly, often
at close range, the better to see
the sudden world as strange. The locality
inhabited the painter and I, decades later,
would be quietly amazed in a gallery
to be acquainted with the many assembled paintings.
At last I recognized and loved the place
Miss Beckett, observed or overheard
with her essential cart, implicatively re-made.
Re-makes—in 1933—indomitably
ignoring the Beaumaris gossips,
with more ease than the male critics
who unlike her pampered, rancorous father
would hardly miss the dowdy woman
by the cliffs in heat or bitter weather.
This route she preferred to the offerings of suitors.
With these words I thank her
for persevering. Yes, repeatedly
there would go the enigmatic, true Miss Beckett
towards her death from exposure, and to a barn,
open to possums and the weather,
most of her paintings stacked
against the day when, decades later,
a sleuth would in dismay see
what might be saved—thereby getting,
as few expected, respect for Clarice Beckett.

Year's End

The neighbours' calendar protrudes from the rubbish bin—
twelve landscape photos in which nothing
went wrong all year, assured as the Earth's

revolution round the Sun. Now another hangs
on their kitchen door, homage
to order. This time last year their dog,

dismembering dolls, was still alive, and other sources
of lamentation had yet to define
a day, a week, a month; each overcome.

How effortlessly one calendar replaces another!
This year it's endangered species above the grid of days,
sent by a righteous niece, each sure to be fingerprint

unique—and, as it happens, for the month
of September, the striped pattern
on the sample zebra—in these conspicuous streets

protected feebly by locks and keys.
Time's the only slippery thief who won't fear
being inked. Or try out a lie, like some time-saving device.

Next May perhaps—the month of the Bengal tiger—like last,
the patriarch will vault the picket fence, camera in hand,
and freeze his raucous family for a captive moment.

Local

To go, set forth, depart,
nick off, skedaddle ...
depending on the temper
of farewell, a wave
given, door wide open.
A century plus since
the Unknown played host
to hero-explorers—
                          who, surely
and most seriously, set forth
into an eventual sweat.

A woman nicks off, springily,
from a desk
and the sedentary life,
endorphins soon cheering
her on but who knows
where the hoped-for lightness
of being might lead, the reptilian
cerebellum, swampland
of the brain, loose about
local geography, the clipped home street
with its spent roses
and fortress fences, the cold
settling in, and on her scale
of stimulating places
approximately bottom
                          yet
on this day, the front gate clicked
shut, suddenly a threshold.

Weight

They loaded the ute
early morning—sunlight
after three damp weeks—the staple
tables, bed, chairs; books
in boxes, five years' worth
of reading condensed
into an impersonal, obedient
weight minus the rejects,
the dumped, the given away.
Clothes, utensils, CDs,
a bike, all there, all
contributing to the buoyant
relief of leaving—the drag
of habituation, its awful
sickening gravity, slackening.
They might have been about
to back out, drive left,
then right, then again left
to clamber into reverse
action only ten minutes hence
or, and why not, got set
to drive along highways
through open, drier country
two thousand miles north
across state borders.
Either would have provided,
in the mirror, a diminishing,
absolutely fine rear view—
as also for astronauts, rising—
clear as their relinquishment,
in spite and because of,
at the now abandoned kitchen
window, the exemplary
fig tree, each year laden,
then lightly speeding into leaf.

Flexibility

Bay of Islands

Not a catastrophe, this,
  since no-one, as it was happening,
    was then available, sedentary, local—

rocks scattered, cataclysmically,
  as here only forces of wind
    and water can shift;

or else some guy does, a re-assembler,
  with a mind to take an excursion
    back through geologic time, stop

in the cold late Pleistocene
  where the coastline now
    is not. Locked once into rock,

the photographed arch that abuts
  the sunny cliff—those
    who pass under it relying

on the firm fact that today
  its inherent collapse
    remains held in play. Everything

recommends implied
  signs for work-in-progress
    or in-regress—flexibility

any way. So, a fine location
  for bipeds to clamber about
    lightly, as it is for a flock

of pied cormorants, atop
    a remainder, sentinel rock,
        to digest their catch. Flexibility

also of tilted and uplifted strata
    in the stacked sequence
        of epochal seasons worth

considering slowly so to wonder,
    in effect—at a flexible stretch—
        what a needle sampling

the geologic record here might
    make of this impressive,
        windswept collection.

As if for the paleontologist
    who to me confessed
        he was deeply into prized fossil

pollen, its music, trapped in layers
    beneath Lake Tanganyika; made refined
        assertions about proto-bees,

surely those making that low note
    a bow might extract from a cello.
        Though what aeolian sediments here

might express I'm only equipped
    to know hearing closely,
        via a flexibly cocked ear, the sea clash

with rock in this irresistible epoch.